Nothing Like the Doll You Learned On

Nothing Like the Doll You Learned On

poems by

Jan Wallace

Cider Press Review
San Diego

NOTHING LIKE THE DOLL YOU LEARNED ON

Copyright © 2020 by Jan Wallace. All rights reserved. No part of this book may be reproduced or utilized in any manner whatsoever without written permission, except in the case of brief quotations embodied in critical articles and reviews. Inquiries should be addressed to:

Cider Press Review

PO BOX 33384

San Diego, CA, 92163

ciderpressreview.com

First edition

10 9 8 7 6 5 4 3 2 1 0

ISBN: 9781930781573

Library of Congress Control Number: 2020931006

Cover Art "Nike of Paionios, Olympia Archaeological Museum" by Carole Raddato, licensed under the Creative Commons Attribution-Share Alike 2.0 Generic license

Book design by Caron Andregg

Winner of the 2019 Cider Press Review Editors' Prize Book Award: ciderpressreview.com/bookaward.

Printed in the United States of America at Bookmobile in Minneapolis, MN USA.

Table of Contents

I Big Blonde Rising

Big Blonde Considers the Nature of Relationships   3
"Let's Invent a Soul Library"   4
Big Blonde's Citation   5
Incident Report   6
My Mother, Endora, and Ereshkigal   7
Witch   8

II Furious Apron

Galaxy   11
Refusing the Moon   12
Near Drowning   13
The Mysterious Country of Knowledge   14
Longing for Rain   15
X-Ray   16
Mouth to Mouth   17
A Possible Theory of Autumn   18

III Country of Our Mothers

Rockets   21
Return to Sender   22
Choir   23
Grave Instruction   24
Aunt Ollie Returns   25
Census Seamstress   26
Whalebone Cottage   27
Looking Glass   28
Surrender   30
Between Worlds   31

IV Entrance to the Animal World

Incarnation   35
Osprey   36
Interior   37
Bird Heart   38
What We Cannot See   39
Sandhill Crane Migration   40
Taking Wing   41
Weather Report   42
What Night Does   43
Even If Danger   44
Horseback   45
Visitation   47
The Mess of Transformation   48
The Passion of Doctor Dixie   49
Memories Stain   50
Accidental Messenger   52
Finally   53
Ornithology Lesson   54

Notes   57

Acknowledgments   59

I

Big Blonde Rising

Big Blonde Considers
the Nature of Relationships

Take the table of elements.
Each born with extra electrons,
electrons to burn, flitting around the face
of sodium, burning a hole in helium's pocket,
so that every element proceeds by casting off.
The noble gases, they don't go begging.

Even the leaves long for, lean toward dirt.
Peer in my petri dish at these yeast cells.
If I excite them, make them fall in love,
they whirl and yield delicate vapors
of longing. When I met him, I saw only his voice,
his dreaming, his umbrella forgotten.
There are scientists who pray
over leaf mold. I'm a simple woman
in a lab coat. The windows here are dirty.
I last saw him on a Thursday.
It rained and he wore a yellow shirt.
The wind could not leave his hat alone.

"Let's Invent a Soul Library"

Scientist on NPR

Big Blonde wants this — the voice, the inflections.
Nothing compared to the scent of the white owl
staring from the Douglas fir at dusk, one red tulip
blooming year after year in the geranium pot.
Big Blonde wants to save all those layers,
the way kids press Silly Putty on newsprint cartoons.
As if the ancestors would not rather swallow
their last sip of tea, leave only ashes and crumbs.

Big Blonde's Citation

Lilies up to my shoulders stain the air with scent.
Wild roses yoke the fence like a too-small bra.
The Department of Inspection
finds you in violation of the Weeds
and Vegetation code.
Butterfly bush bursts sidewalk cracks.
Fireweed rockets rain up.
Neighbors complain the wild display
encroaches the sidewalk.
That woman takes up too much space.
She'd better watch out.
Calling attention to herself like that.

Incident Report

When the guy got his skull
bashed on my front porch I worried
my Navajo drag queen roommate
might upset my mother.
Shut that pretty man down.
No stilettos. No make-up.
Made him swear off pot.
Even cleaned the oven.
Bad block, he says smoking
with my mother. Cigarette
clenched in the corner of
her mouth, she mops
blood from my front stoop.
You were never tidy.

My Mother, Endora, and Ereshkigal

In Suburban Seattle in the 60s
we had no Underworld.
We had no Queen of Heaven.
We had Bewitched.
Samantha of the magical
and her dopey consort Darren.
Endora of the flowing caftans
and regal glamor.
It was witch on witch.
My mother loved jade
and gems, smoked Salems.
In that Sumerian myth, Ereshkigal,
the Queen of Heaven's
twisted sister, shreds her,
rends her, to keep her under.
My mother and Ereshkigal
make a good team.
Ereshkigal pumps the hell-hot
bellows, my mother
aims the steam. Give me some old-time
Sumerians. Give me Queens.
Lay me down at the unutterable altar,
dig the burnished gemstone
from this honey shot mess,
this sparking ember nest,
where it takes me.

Witch

We knew she was a witch. She lived alone in that red house almost at the end of the trail through the woods to Brookside Elementary. Smell of peat and cedar. White oyster mushrooms sticking out of hemlock like ears. Avoid the nettles, calves bare above ankle socks. Muddy saddle shoes. Three-legged black dog. Shotgun leaning on the front porch. She wore pants. Girls wear dresses. She wore pants and men's shirts. We just knew.

There is a woman who lives on the corner on my street, now. Overgrown yard. Political signs blooming, liberal, outdated. Drives a diesel pick up. Hangs a cigarette from her lip, walks a tiny dog named Bruiser. Tosses peanuts to crows who follow. Hummingbirds nest in overgrown wicker baskets hanging on her porch.

My next-door neighbor canes her way over. Grump. Grump. Sits down to gas off—leans both arms on her three-legged cane like a podium. Says shooting stars are astronaut poop. Curses the rose bush out back, all the green apples. *Woman on the corner,* she says, *mark my words, is a god damned witch.*

II

Furious Apron

Galaxy

Ancients thought honey fell from rising stars,
never believed bees could gather nectar
from earthly constellations: forsythia,
lilac, the dome of rhododendrons
crossing a muddy path, each ring
of petals a sustenance cup.
The scout returns pollen-stained,
reeking of peach, of lavender.
We, too, have scouts.
Radio. Telescope. We comb the heavens
listening for a sound like our own,
a friend across the fence.
A hum in our ear. All we hear
is ourselves, 20 years ago. Walter Cronkite,
I Love Lucy returning echoes. Electric scrape
of light and distance.

Refusing the Moon

I don't want to go to the moon. I would miss eating tomatoes—
especially heirloom. Green Zebra, meaty Purple Russians.
On the moon, there are no Gold Rush Currents,
or rhododendrons brash and red as Cancan dancers.
But back to tomatoes—
I would miss Jubilee's heavy, yielding golden fruit,
legendary Mortgage Lifters roasted slow with salt and oil.
Long distance the earth's cold, a blue marble, no fair trade
for Auroras cooked slow and sweet in dusky vinegar. Best
to sink my teeth into the weighty flesh of swallowed sun.

Near Drowning

This is when I was very young and still enchanted. I was not a real child. I was a thing of imagination. In the summer, my family rented a cabin by Lake Huron which we shared with our cousins. In those days, when I set my gaze on the lawn falling away toward the horizon, I became the green, I became the vanishing edge. If I looked long enough at a robin hopping for worms I became the full little belly breast, I became the fluff of feathers. There was not enough to keep me inside my body, to keep my feet in my saltwater sandals climbing down the 97 stairs from the landing to the hot sand on the beach. When my older cousins walked out into the cool lake, I followed. I stared out where the water met the sky lip, where clouds sat their bottoms down and doubled in reflection. My toes met wet sand as I walked one pudgy four-year old leg in front of the other heading deeper and deeper. Until I was looking up at the edge of the water from below, the lens distorted. I remember seeing the light just under the water's surface, a perfect moment, and the sudden hand of my uncle under my armpit, as I got hauled out into yelling air and clamor. I held that brief, perfect silence in my mind like a hard candy in my cheek. Private, and sweet, and wholly my own.

The Mysterious Country of Knowledge

When Dr. Whiting, his zipper down, fly wide open,
lorded over us with cosines and variables,
I never raised a hand. His stuffy steam-heated
after-lunch room was principal domain.
The place where unknown quantities could be
replaced, where integers were infinite,
equations elliptic.
Seniors smoked to Jimi Hendrix
in the lounge, David Cooper stuck his tongue
in my mouth. I didn't believe in sex or astronauts.
Or that billion-dollar bridges
would carry us. Forced to the board,
I'd scratch X and Y wildly until chaos
looked like formulas. I was going for cosmetics,
holding hands with Cooper.
Whiting was never fooled. He made me stand
probing renegade numbers for solutions.
I arrived at the sort of sadness poverty makes.
Coins not equal to a bag of potatoes,
a well-meaning dearth.

Longing for Rain

Because a small part of the brain has given up,
the blind man has lost his eye's name for things.
He leans toward a woman, hearing thin wrists.
Behind his eyes a red-haired girl
in a doorway, waving good-bye.
At ten, losing sight in the left,
he said good-bye to his shoulder.
Trusts the mirror to save him.
And because his body is missing,
he believes in lips and fingertips,
a sort of topography of bone and muscle.
And as for the woman, if he eases
his palm down the spoon of her belly, leans
against her breast, he can hear her ticking.
When the blind man opens his front door
he knows fourteen steps take him into the world.
But a kite caught in an elm, the clatter
of a stroller, three houses down,
one passing car and he must count
out loud to keep the walk straight.
If it rains, oh if it rains
he can hear where lawn begins.
Rain holds the house down.
Holds the shape of eyelids
so the blind man can sleep.

X-Ray

The man who mothered X-rays
turned everything
inside out. He could not love
what he could not uncover.
His wife watched the laboratory door
swing shut every day.
Even Christmas. On her birthday
he asked her in, laid her
out on his table like a gem.
The woman held shock still
as the man moved
his machine. For her blood
the man presented her
with her own bones.
Ashen, luminous, empty.

Mouth to Mouth

With every breath, we entertain
molecules used by Hedy Lamarr and your dentist.
Scientists look for signs of life
in old air stalled in Civil War buttons,
pyramids, glaciers, cannons
buried in dirt. They love the smell
of frozen bubbles, prying for tomb-air.
It's not pretty. We're intimate
as drinking buddies. I can quit
mourning my old lovers. They're here
all right, old cigarette breath, toothpaste.
In lifeguard class, they show how to bring
a doll to life. In resuscitation, we clear
an air path, a wind tunnel to send
our breath into darkness. The blue boy
before you, wet sand on his lips, is nothing
like the doll you learned on.
Move his heavy tongue.
Pray he'll be seduced
by this secondhand brew.

A Possible Theory of Autumn

Maybe it's sugar that turns the leaves.
In school they said movement
and loss, oval spin unraveling light behind
so the sun is thinner, diminishing like a ball of yarn.
And the leaves dying. Fever flush. Scientists insist
sugar has been falling down
the body all year long, thickening the ankles
slowing the pulse, so what's left in the leaves
upstairs is a thin chlorophyll throb –
This year the trees have gone crimson, gold and pale —
drenched, bruised and unfolding.
Less a leaving than a lingering.

III

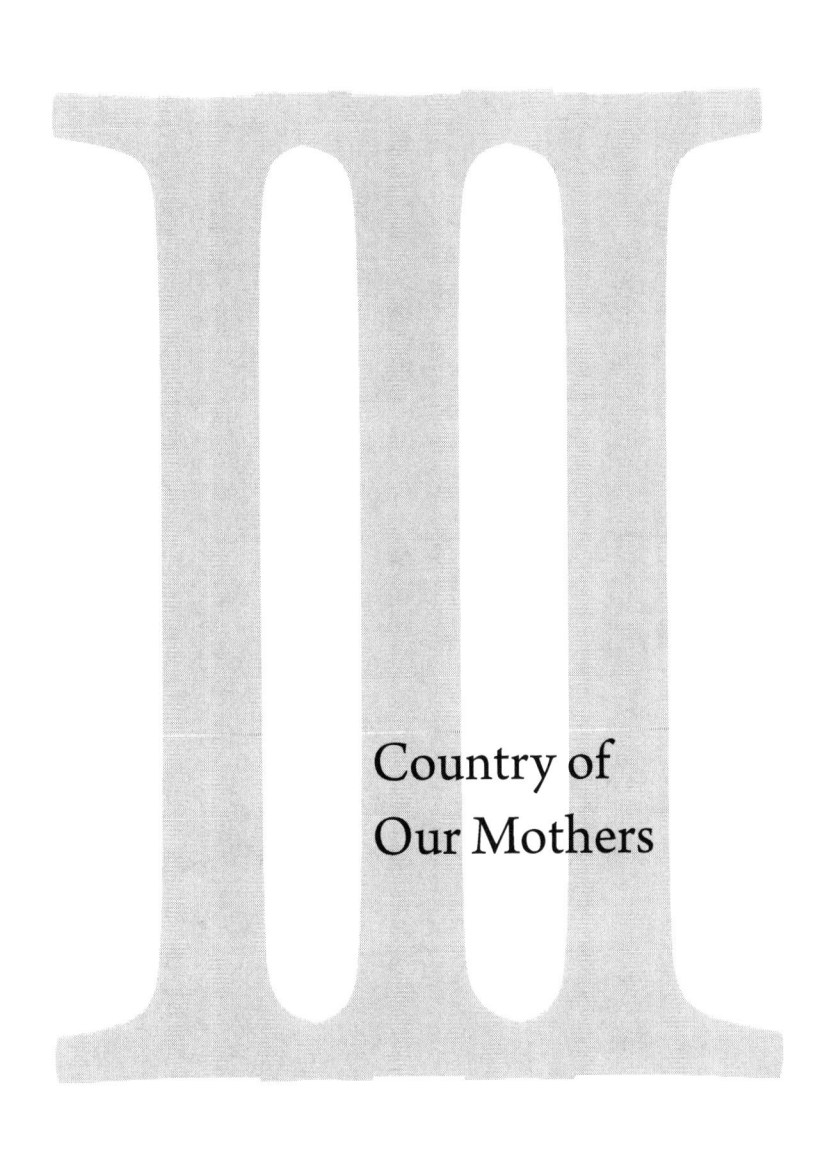

Country of
Our Mothers

Rockets

The woman on TV watched scientists freeze her mother's head.
"I didn't want to lose her," she said.
What a nice container the skull makes,
a traveling case for the brain, tidy satchel
of person. The essence of say,
your mother: apron and sharp tongue,
coral PTA lipstick. Let those experts
freeze her head, Winter Wheat
hairdo and all, and you will always have her.

When a body breaks down, when the skin unzips,
the lung and liver come out with the secrets
of floured hands fretting like birds.
Bright lights of autopsy dismiss spleen and tangled
entrails, bucket the heart: in and out as she napped
that last afternoon, as if four chambers
signify nothing more.

Prize the brain, believe it contains
your electric mother in gelatinous filigree,
trace details trapped in impulse
like your grade school hand-print ashtray,
or the way a river knocks its banks in,
swallowing silt, crying forward.

Return to Sender

In the end, each one leaves the body like a puppet dress
that's lost its magic. Nobody knows what to do with ashes.
There are rules and guidelines: if you're scattering
remains beware of breezes, do not wear lip gloss.
There will be chunks of bone. The Medical Examiner's
shelves crowd with the unclaimed. Rusty tin urn
with hearts and roses found in a suitcase in a Walmart
parking lot, ashes left at the airport, on a Greyhound bus,
on the steps of the Methodist Chapel. Remains sent
to a daughter's last known address
arrived marked Return to Sender.
Everybody else died first. Or nobody
cared. Today the Examiner will scatter orphan
ashes over Puget Sound and the sky
will only almost ever rain—

Choir

The man in line at the IGA drags
a thought balloon behind him.
Inside it I see a photographic negative
of a woman in a straw hat
standing in the rain.
A baby hovers
just about the bank teller's left shoulder.
The infant is not crying. The cop stopped at the corner
has a guy who is not there riding shotgun.
There is a cat-sized hole
in my sky: black ruff; imperial tail ascending.
The no-more cat follows me past the saltbox
corner church where they always sing in Latin.
We pass pale blue Mother Mary
blessing lilac blossoms that weep perfume.
It is Tuesday. The sun has fallen. Choir practices
upstairs behind thick windows gone lavender.
The walls cannot contain the ribbons—
that man's straw-hat lady, the cop's last partner.
That bank teller's child. My gone cat. All gone to choir.

Grave Instruction

Someone I admired, famous among poets and lovers
of poetry, is buried in a fancy graveyard
where our city founders rest beside the sister of the Indian Chief
they hoodwinked for the land. When I was in Scotland,
staying at the castle, sleeping on a scratchy
horsehair bed—in that ancient place meant to be a writer's retreat
but which, in November, was one long Victorian ghost story,
I ate my lunch alone in the local cemetery.
A grave is like a little boat that has run finally aground.
I like to think of a cocktail party, everybody freed
from the body's concerns, from vanity, "my earlobes are growing
as I get older" my friend complained.
One fan taped the poet's own words to her stone:
"You have come to the shore.
There are no instructions."

Aunt Ollie Returns

There must be quite a throng up there by now.
All the friends tossed from speeding cars,
suddenly small as footballs, or squeezed out
of life by some renegade molecule going wild
in the blood. I imagine them, the dead, all piled up
like Keystone Cops behind the big sky wall,
listening with a glass, eavesdropping
on our clumsy lives. Here's dead Aunt Ollie.
She's on the hood of your Dodge
nattering, with her false teeth out,
tossing her glass eye hand to hand
like she used to do at dinner. Plain as day
and twice as loud she advises you on driving.
"Step on it," as you quiver down the on-ramp.
You press down on that pedal, zipping into traffic.
Aunt Ollie, hair flying, pressed against the hood
spread eagle like Jesus on the cross,
"Well done, girl, now join us."

Census Seamstress

Violet takes pity on the foreigner,
warms up her microfiche machine.
She steers sure as a seamstress
across three census years
like the open field of pillowcase,
straight shot, fingers pucker and free
fabric beneath the needle.
She holds a pen in her teeth like a pin.
Violet knows Sugarhouse Road,
Menzies Close, the seven children
all factory workers, two infant deaths, ink notations.
But she goes on past tea time,
working the pedal in that dark office.
She's sewing a dress so complex,
wild red hair, hand-me-down shoes,
cast iron pot steaming. The lost tangle
of voices released in pleats and folds.

Whalebone Cottage

We are this close—I could wear her dress,
smell her long gone perfume in the folds
of muslin. Shudder, a breeze, a sensible
word in my ear. Time leaves the glass
where our eyes match a hundred years apart.
Whalebone held her belly down, a horsehair
bustle rose behind her like the moon.
The hourglass architecture of promise,
hips and breasts—landmarks for a man so far
at sea he believes his dream. Holding a pillow
in the shape his good wife makes
with her whalebone and her bustle.
The flannel and wool, stays and ribbons a house
for her body. She was his vaulted rotunda,
his sanctuary. Ribs and window, mouth
and wrist, twilled calico or crinoline—
widow walk heart cradled
in whalebone or tendered in the palm of silk.

Looking Glass

Even this far from home
on a train from Inverness
a familiar face below the window.
Dusk and rain, the moving crowd,
I thought I knew him. The train pulled away
just as I rapped my knuckle on the glass.
That's how it was with my great grandmother.
Angular and tall, skinny as a schoolmarm
she pulled her hair back as if she could organize
her temper. Her husband came and went
in a wooden ship. Gone by the time
the child would be born.
The census man taxed her for her window.
Some bricked themselves in rather than pay.
She kept the little eye open squinting
at cobblestones and gulls. Sea air seeped
into her heavy dresses, perfume lingered
in her cuffs. Even her golden chain
smelled of roses, musk and soup bones.
She wore the dingy walls like a mantle.
At night, she'd scrub everything
within an inch of its life. This is what her kids
would remember: any nonsense at the table
and you got a crack with a wooden spoon.
I want to understand how we can vanish.
When I had a lover, the longer
we spent dreaming the more we'd
twist down that dark helix river.
When my great grandma dreamt by the fire,
she'd poke an iron tongue in the coals
to see outside the granite walls,

the man in his fusty woolens,
the ship moving away, disappearing,
embers falling like a storm.
When I walked the long, muddy trail to the ruin
I tore my skirt on a bramble,
muddied my stockings. I could hear my mother:
"Just look at yourself."

Surrender

I am emptying my chest onto the lawn,
turning my house inside out. Antique lace,
silken camisoles, slips thin as skin
hung where they don't belong.

I held his hand for hours, I could not see
how he could empty himself from his body.
How his skin could let him go.
I thought that trick, that turning
is how the dead know.

There's smoke over the crematory,
a little wind fills with rain,
there was a man on the couch
with morphine counting his way down.

Air so wet it spatters, rain riven
gowns and negligees—weather changes
silk, the feel, the hue.
How can a body let go like that?
Into hunger that sweeps up and pushes under.

I told him everything slow,
from the beginning,
as if the story would keep him. Words to burn.
White slips on the lawn, turning
myself inside out.

Between Worlds

Dragonflies ply the sky regular as punctuation these hot days
patrolling solo, or double-decker like bi-planes. The hummingbird

hovers in a maple thicket outside my window peering in.
Atmosphere so wet and thick it is not air, not liquid.

My mother was already most of the way out of her mind
when she said she tasted perfume on her teeth.

Still in this world but not of it, remembering
an invented life in the fabulous scents of Paris.

This bird wings her pulse-pocket body aloft.
Curious spirit, scouting for sugar or emissary.

IV

Entrance to the
Animal World

Incarnation

A falconer raises the deadliest of birds, the goshawk,
after an enormous loss. The falconer is soft hearted
toward the bleeding rabbits, the blood-struck pheasants,
and toward the goshawk, Mabel.
A fractured foot hobbles me in a black boot.
I miss walks around the lake to spy birds hunting.
Red meat helps my bone heal faster. Chew for marrow.
Chew for bone. I live with a calico. She'd savage
a mouse in a second. The falconer pulled out
of grief through life with a feathered sniper,
their gritty hunting forays the living shape.

Osprey

Estuary expert, elegant fisherman, head turning
within feathered armor. His claws reverse
to carry a fish headfirst. Lethal specialist,
brilliant with splash and fin. How did he come
to rest in this fishless pasture?

He let me look at his ruffled neck, hooked beak,
specks and fleas. Probably he was on his way
to Panama when the magnet in his pigeon head blinked
forgetting how the air should feel—
now water, the diving rush for cool food is nowhere
and he is homesick with hunger. No, he is his hunger.
Yellow eyes scan the grass for a mouse, a blind vole.
Anything this pasture offers will not be right.

A monarch sat, wings clasped back,
in the middle of Shake Rag Road.
I tried to help, turned him upside down.
Maybe I should have left him mining
nectar from asphalt.

I remember kissing. Clear and cold, Lake Cain lapped
old wooden posts beneath us. The man's hands
under my shirt. His neck like leftover sun.
We were each other's wrong place to rest.

It was October then, as it is now. The horizon
spills gold sideways over rusty fields.
Dried stalks of summer corn rustle like ghosts.
This time of year, we know
night licks the world clean.

Interior

I haven't seen your woodstove
have not warmed socks wet
from running through long grass
chasing after a feral cat. My sweater
has not hung across the back
of a deep red armchair.
The thick indoor scent of wet wool,
burning cedar, none of that drifts.
Rain-soaked smoky air cannot remind
me of the Coleman lantern
under the dripping tarp when we got to stay
up late playing cards, the satisfying snap
of cribbage. I am not thinking of the moth-white
center of the light, its kerosene smell, or how
we could not shake the lantern, shatter
the miraculous, gauzy sack.

Bird Heart

Frost cracked the terra cotta birdhouse,
its bear-shaped face too high to rescue
reminds and reminds, here is something I can't fix.
I don't know if sparrows care
if walls let light in. A pair came by
inspecting branch and tree, poked
with nervous beaks and twitched away.
A house holds what it can: dried moss,
cracked leaves, a few strands of golden, stolen hair.
If sky cracks in, a bird must remember
wind against lilacs, the screen door slamming,
every outside indication of more.
Imagine the field inside
a sparrow's vision speeding out,
a backwards moving lens letting
landscape in. The bluebells' determined
march over pansies, the spell
clematis casts climbing ivy
like limbs tangled up in love.
The sparrow's field would have to hold
the slow stone path past fence and mailbox,
the way loss arrives disguised as letter.
Your card was like that.
I could not reply.
You left like a storm that stopped.
I thought last year's couple might return—
but I don't know about the
bravery of sparrows.

What We Cannot See

We can't see the fires from here. Smoke smudges the sun
and blurs the horizon. We follow the Sammamish, a river
that has all but given up, barely braiding forward
in rivulets toward the lake's lap. This dry season's
left the water low, tinged with copper.
We pedal, pausing to watch the heron.
Up to his knobby knees in silt,
he shakes his fusty feathers in
the caliginous heat as he picks up one skeletal leg,
shifting in the slimy weeds like an old man
with bed hair performing his ablutions.
In the best muck he freezes, gazing
down as he did yesterday,
as he will do again tomorrow.
He believes in unseen fish or frogs.
Just as we in our haze must
trust the promised rain.

Sandhill Crane Migration

Southern Arizona, February 2015.
Birdwatchers blow through tinny towns
with one good ice cream shop
and no public bathroom
halting at Border Patrol checkpoints
to answer men whose guns
ride level with drivers' chins
and speed to gather at the far shore of
Whitewater Draw.
Cranes appear in perfect formation
under the sun-exhausted sky.
Elegant fowl, sleek and grey, they're tall
as Victorian ladies.
Feathery bustles tucked under, they hobnob
on the far bank of the draw, each
crane topped with a crimson cap.
They're back for a wet dabble
after feasting in trampled fields
for the comfort of Sandhill roaring cries.
The cranes know where they've been.
They know where they're going.
The watchers will get lost on their way home.

Taking Wing

Yard as altar,
ancient liberal slogans,
armpit high crabgrass,
one basket brims
with blossoms, crippled wicker.
She pulls up,
smoke stuck to lower lip, parks
the diesel. "Come see,"
gruff invite. Broken gate,
crowded porch, she points
to her resident crow, broken
foot. I offer nuts from my pocket, no,
she lets him beak a cheeseburger.
Shows me the hummingbirds' nest
in the dead vines—
thimble entry into heaven.

Weather Report

1
Confused duck, I thought, *sitting so high
in the drowned-root tree.* No, it's a heron.
None of us wearing our glasses, we squint.
Others stop to ask what they cannot see.
Last week an eagle perched
in a front yard drawing a crowd like this.

2
Shawl of rain after wide-open wind and sun.
The seal pup should be shy, yet hauls his sea
body up on the dock next to the soggy, lost red glove.
A seal fin rubs an eye as we watch
gathered like doting aunts. Official Seal Watchers
say he'll move on soon.
Why this is so hard to bear.

3
Peanut in beak the crow aims his shoe-shine
black eyes right at mine. *No more,* I say shaking
the bag. For the crow, I am marked. One with nuts.
One with what he needs. Seal. Eagle. Crow.
I think I am beginning to see.

What Night Does

Flicker mother beats her wings
against the patch where my
neighbor walled her nest in.
Hushed crows stand vigil over one
taken down by rat poison.
But the flicker persists,
crows return to their evening
perch like weather.
Anyone would swallow
the moon raw and go nova.

Even If Danger

She wanted a drink,
that raccoon, from my backyard
bird bath. She ducked
behind wild violets,
peeked over top.
I snapped a shot.
Back in the Midwest,
a raccoon snared
in a live trap
meant for feral cats
raged against metal.
My neighbor took him—
one bullet.
Tossed the body
from his moving car.
Raccoons live under
my friend's houseboat
staging opera all night long.
We feed them kibbles.
Zorro eyes hold mine, little claw
paw searching my palm.
They don't look at the food,
just at danger, even if
danger is what feeds them.

Horseback

I was ten—Western. English
horseback lessons,
my big black trotter, mine for the hour,
down the back road
under ash and fir.
Cool air like swimming
a lake current, a drift I'd pass my toes through,
a place I could get lost.
I rode the Appaloosa
bareback to prove I could.
Out of the blue, she jumped the fence.
Wind knocked out of me.
I think of Horse Heaven Hills
rising and falling,
mist resting in the valley
is the mane of a ghost horse.
Or standing horses grazing,
meadowed horses standing.
Or winter horses.
Snow and fog, the whole world
the color of bone.
And I turn.
The great chest emerges,
a breathing shadow,
sudden shudder of animal.
Big brown eyes.
Slow pulse. Look. I want to be easy
as that horse. Settled in.
Saddle of hips.
Smoothed out forehead.
Calm and secret.

I can't sleep tonight. Wind rides
the empty reservoir
outside my building,
banging, my loose door.
My open window.
The back of the horse
is the back of the ridge,
and back of the ridge is the sky,
and what escapes me,
what is let loose is sinew
and heat, muscle and bone,
serious horse pulling
my frantic heart.

Visitation

The spotted mare, skinny with age
and her brown quarter horse companion
stood framed between gingham curtains.

The old farmer asked how those two horses
—long passed on
could be standing in the paddock nuzzling.

To see his friends in the liquid spring air
the man had to know where the mare's muzzle
had gone gray. Had to have brushed
each horse's withers on a dusty hot day
after digging caked dirt from their frogs.
He had to have watched hard as they flicked flies
and lipped carrots from the neighbor girl's hand.
He had to have watched so fiercely he drew them back.

The Mess of Transformation

Perhaps the hunter admired
the deer, how she leapt through
Castle Rock Valley easy as a wave
on water. But only part of his arrow
remained in her side: her neck
bent wrong, muzzle distorted,
suckled teats snail swarmed.
Imperfectly she lay beneath cedar,
legs tucked under like a cat.
It took three women to ease her onto a blanket ,
surprised by how hard it is to handle a body.
Crows marked the morning, soaking up light,
cawing it back between gun shots. The air
smelled of nothing—cold stops musk, the scent
of rotting nurse logs. But the doe reeked
with the mess of transformation.
To track her, adore
her scat. Her impossibly brown eyes,
not glassy but maple syrup, would
have seen us struggle with the weight
of what he left.
He would be glad to know
she lies buried under sandstone with
rose petals, tobacco
and an apple for the other world.

The Passion of Doctor Dixie

Consider the sad lepidopterist
leaping after butterflies for a whiff
of passing swallowtail, the sweetbrier
siren of clouded yellow.
Not for him the great field
of rolling and holding, the dull
weight of flesh, hot breath
of human crooning loud and ungraceful.
The scent's a seduction tool.
Fritillaries stir the breeze
with the scent of sandalwood,
vanilla—secret odors Dixie discovers
rubbing a finger down the tufted abdomen
or barely brushing a lower wing.
Some smell of kitchen sink
and cabbage water, and some betray
a taste for rot and excrement.
Once he caught a whiff like pig sties,
he could not believe anything
so small could smell so much.
But a man can forgive a butterfly
its secret passions, its tremoring
energies stinking only for love.

Memories Stain

Just at dusk light reels away
drenching dead grass in gold.
Crows tease cats
from the vine maple.
*Morphine makes roses
even deeper,* my dying
friend said. I imagine
a paper flower unfolding
the bruise, undoing.

I pick at the hem of twilight,
as if day were a long silk skirt
fashioned to suit me,
wide as afternoon, sunken blue
as that last swallow of sun.

The house I grew up in is filled
with strangers. They burn toast,
boys roughhouse past bedtime.
I think I left something there
in the wall. I think I hid
letters written in lemon juice.

I sat on the porch last year,
bare legs, ankles freezing,
ignoring autumn. Still the bird
of panic rose in my chest, the way
my lungs close like fists,
dark comes faster and faster.
At eight I baby-sat a goat.
A coyote ripped its throat,

blood a shock of ribbon.
I found its fallen body tethered
in wild strawberries.
They all said it wasn't my fault.
Even paid me fifty cents.
I wonder if we leave our selves
in the air or a little higher.

Accidental Messenger

The seal pup dozes, fat belly, at the water's edge.
On the dock above, people snap pics.
Wet sand lapping, drizzle and haze
familiar as skin to the seal. To us, he's exotic.
He is not of our wooden-chair,
clunky-bodied world. We stand
in our hard shoes on our own toes—
leaning into a trance
filling ourselves with our own dark story.

We cannot touch,
just admire his spotted, sleek self, dapper fins.
Most days I scan the waters of the Sound for a telltale nose,
hoping, I have to believe the seals are there, hidden.
But once in a while this: a seal pup resting
—messenger reminding of us what we cannot name but know.

Finally

That was the autumn one adolescent
buck broke with his skittish rituals
and stood in bald-faced daylight
helping himself to tomatoes and basil.

The tall grass on the prairie became so many bonfires.
The crabapples grown so
full they could not sustain
their swinging and plopped
one by one
onto the flattened path where four deer
and one fox had passed.

If we could hear red
it would resound like stone towers,
the ravine, cathedral
leaves and bells.

Ornithology Lesson

It's an act of desperation,
the rare mating ritual
of the bald eagle pair

come together mid-air between
mountains. You can barely make
them out, you with your Audubon

binoculars. The two of them
bound beak and feather,
claw and wing, having taken

leave of every other
instinct. Mostly what they
have forgotten is how to breathe.

They drop their wings,
their full weight washed clean
by the thick true wash of lust—

which brings every creature right
out of the wild kingdom into the one common
denominator. Aren't you glad,

bird watchers, you're not a part
of that? Those eagles risk it all
for the long swallow of sex,

and just when you know this must
be a suicide pact, just before they hit
the earth and scatter like burst pillows –

And there you are, binoculars around
your ankles, as the eagles pick up
the next feathering breeze.

NOTES

"My Mother, Endora, and Ereshkigal": Ereshkigal is Queen of the Underworld in the ancient Sumerian myth of Inanna. Endora is a character from *Bewitched*, which is an American television sitcom fantasy series, originally broadcast for eight seasons on ABC from September 17, 1964, to March 25, 1972.

"Longing for Rain" is for John M. Hull who wrote *Touching The Rock, An Experience of Blindness.*

"X-Ray": The first image Wilhelm Roentgen made using x-rays in 1895 was that of his wife's hand. She later died of radiation sarcoma.

"Grave Instruction" is for Denise Levertov who is interred in Lakeview Cemetery, Seattle, WA. The quoted line is from her poem, "The Book Without Words," from *A Door in the Hive*, page 44.

"Looking Glass" is for my great grandmother, Elspet Landry, Aberdeen, Scotland, 1842-1918.

"Surrender" is for Grey Lambert, 1958-1991.

"Incarnation" was written after reading *H is for Hawk* by Helen Macdonald.

"What We Cannot See" is about the Okanogan fires in August 2015, the biggest in Washington state history.

ACKNOWLEDGMENTS

"Longing for Rain" and "Ornithology Lesson" have previously appeared in *Poetry Northwest*

"Surrender" has previously appeared in *Field*

"Autumnal" has previously appeared in *Nimrod*

"Mouth to Mouth" has previously appeared in *A Fine Madness*

"Rockets" has previously appeared in *Hubbub*

"Sandhill Crane Migration," "Finally," and "Osprey" have previously appeared in *Terrain.org: A Journal of the Built* and *Natural Environments*

"Cemetery" has previously appeared in *Off Paper*, The Project Room's Literary Journal.

Some of these poems were completed during a residency at Hawthornden Castle, International Writer's Retreat, Scotland. I would like to thank that institution for its generosity.